AVERY WRIGHT

AI and the Art of Binary

Contents

1

Introduction

Explanation of A.I. and Binary

In the field of artificial intelligence (A.I.), binary is a critical component that plays a vital role in the functioning and development of intelligent systems. Understanding binary is crucial for anyone working with A.I. or interested in exploring its applications and advancements.

Definition of A.I. and its applications

A.I. is a broad field that encompasses a range of technologies and techniques used to create systems that can perform tasks typically requiring human-like intelligence. This can include tasks such as image recognition, speech recognition, decision-making, and natural language processing.

Explanation of binary and its role in computing

Binary, on the other hand, is a system of numbering that uses only two digits, 0 and 1. It is the language that computers use to process and store information. Binary is an essential building block of computing, and it is the basis for the functioning of all computer systems, including those used in A.I.

Importance of Understanding Binary in A.I.

Binary as the foundation of A.I.

Binary is the foundation of A.I. and plays a crucial role in its functioning. A.I. relies on binary code to process, store, and communicate information. Binary code consists of only two digits, 0 and 1, which represent electrical signals or on/off states in computing.

3

Benefits of understanding binary for the development and deployment of A.I.

Having a good understanding of binary is essential for those involved in the development and deployment of A.I. technologies. It helps in coding, debugging, and optimizing A.I. systems, and enables better communication with other A.I. professionals. Understanding binary also helps in making informed decisions about the ethical and societal implications of A.I. development and deployment.

A.I. and Binary: A Match Made in Computing A. Explanation of how binary and A.I. work together

Binary the language of computers

Binary the language of computers and A.I. systems, allows for efficient processing and storage of data. In A.I., binary is used to represent the inputs and outputs of algorithms and to store data in a machine-readable format. It plays a critical role in allowing A.I. systems to make decisions, learn from data, and solve problems.

By representing data in binary format, A.I. algorithms can perform mathematical operations and comparisons on large amounts of data quickly and accurately. This allows for the development of sophisticated A.I. systems, such as machine learning algorithms, that can analyze vast amounts of data and make predictions with high accuracy.

Overall, binary and A.I. work together to allow for the efficient processing and analysis of data, enabling the development of advanced A.I. technologies.

How binary is used to represent and process data in A.I. systems

Binary plays a critical role in A.I. systems, as it is the foundation for representing and processing data. When an A.I. system processes information, it does so by breaking down data into binary code, a series of 0s and 1s that can be easily processed by computers. This allows the system to make decisions and perform actions based on the data that is input.

The role of binary in enabling A.I. algorithms to make decisions and perform actions

A.I. algorithms use binary to make decisions by comparing the values of various parameters and determining which is the most relevant or accurate. For example, a machine learning algorithm might use binary to process large amounts of data and identify patterns and correlations. The binary code is then used to make predictions and decisions based on that information.

Binary is also used to represent and process data in A.I. systems. For example, images and audio files can be processed and analyzed as binary code, allowing the system to identify features and patterns that might not be noticeable to the human eye or ear. This information can then be used to make decisions and take actions, such as recognizing an object in an image or translating speech into text.

Examples of A.I. applications powered by binary

Machine learning algorithms

Machine learning algorithms are one of the most prominent A.I. applications powered by binary. These algorithms use binary to analyze data, identify patterns, and make predictions. For example, binary is used to represent the data that is fed into a machine learning algorithm, such as a decision tree or a neural network. The algorithm then uses this binary data to learn, make decisions, and improve over time.

Natural language processing

Another important application of binary in A.I. is natural language processing. Binary is used to process and analyze text and speech data, enabling A.I. systems to understand and generate human-like speech. For example, binary is used to represent words, sentences, and even entire documents, which are then processed by A.I. algorithms to identify patterns and meaning. This enables natural language processing A.I. systems to translate between languages, summarize text, and respond to questions.

Computer vision

Computer vision is another area where binary plays a crucial role. Binary is used to represent image and video data, which is then processed by A.I. algorithms to identify objects, patterns,

6

and scenes. For example, binary is used to represent pixel data, which is then processed by computer vision algorithms to identify and track objects, detect patterns, and perform image and video analysis. This enables computer vision A.I. systems to perform tasks such as object recognition, facial recognition, and even autonomous navigation

The significance of binary in enabling A.I. technologies

Binary, the language of computers, plays a crucial role in enabling the development and deployment of artificial intelligence technologies. In this chapter, we will explore the significance of binary in the world of A.I. and why it is an essential component of modern A.I. systems.

Binary as the Backbone of A.I. Systems

Binary is the backbone of A.I. systems, allowing for high-speed and efficient processing. This is because computers and A.I. systems are designed to understand and process information in binary form. By representing data as a series of 0s and 1s, binary enables A.I. systems to process large amounts of information quickly and accurately.

Binary in Advanced A.I. Technologies

Binary is also a crucial component in the development of advanced A.I. technologies, such as deep learning and reinforcement learning. These technologies rely on complex algorithms that are capable of processing vast amounts of data and making decisions based on that data. Binary is the foundation for these algorithms, enabling them to process data at high speeds and make decisions with high accuracy.

Binary and the Physical World

Finally, binary plays a critical role in allowing A.I. systems to interact with the physical world through robotics and other technologies. By using binary to communicate and control robotic systems, A.I. technologies are able to perform a wide range of physical tasks, such as manufacturing, transportation, and even surgery.

2

The Basics of Binary

I. Introduction

A. Overview of the chapter

This chapter provides an introduction to the basics of binary, including its definition, explanation, and applications. It also covers the importance of understanding binary in the field of Artificial Intelligence (A.I.).

B. Importance of understanding binary in A.I.

Binary plays a critical role in the field of A.I. as it is the underlying foundation of computer hardware and software. Understanding binary is essential for those looking to work in A.I. as it is used in data representation and processing, algorithms and models, and a variety of A.I. applications, such as image recognition, natural language processing, and robotics.

II. Definition and Explanation of Binary

A. Explanation of binary

1. Definition of binary

Binary is a numerical system that uses only two digits, 0 and 1, to represent data and information.

2. Explanation of binary digits (bits) and binary numbers

A binary digit, or bit, is the smallest unit of information in binary, representing either 0 or 1. Binary numbers are sequences of bits that can be combined to represent values ranging from zero to a maximum value determined by the number of bits.

3. Overview of binary operations

In binary, operations such as addition, subtraction, multiplication, and division can be performed using only 0s and 1s. These operations are carried out using binary arithmetic, which is a set of rules that govern how binary numbers are manipulated.

B. Applications of binary

1. Binary in computer hardware

Binary is used in computer hardware to control and communicate between different components, such as the CPU, memory, and storage.

2. Binary in software

Binary is also used in software to store and process data, as well as to represent characters, images, and audio.

III. How Binary Works in A.I.

A. Explanation of binary in A.I.

1. Binary in data representation and processing

In A.I., binary is used to represent and process data in a way that computers can understand. This allows for the efficient storage and manipulation of large amounts of data, which is critical for A.I. applications such as image recognition and natural language processing.

2. Binary in algorithms and models

Binary is also used in the development of A.I. algorithms and models, providing a framework for the creation of sophisticated machine learning algorithms that can learn from and make predictions based on data.

B. Examples of A.I. applications powered by binary

1. Image recognition

Binary is used in image recognition applications to process and analyze images, enabling computers to identify and categorize objects, people, and scenes.

2. Natural language processing

Binary is also used in natural language processing applications to process and understand human language, allowing for tasks such as text classification and sentiment analysis.

3. Robotics

Binary is used in robotics to control and coordinate the movements of robots, allowing them to perform tasks and interact with their environment.

IV. The Relationship between Binary and Computer Science

A. Explanation of how binary is central to computer science

Binary is central to computer science as it forms the basis of how computers store and process information. Without binary, computers would not be able to perform the operations required to execute software and carry out A.I. applications.

B. Overview of the role of binary in computer architecture

In computer architecture, binary plays a critical role in determining the structure and organization of computer systems. This includes the design of memory and storage systems, as well as the communication between different components within a computer. The use of binary allows for efficient and precise representation of information, which is necessary for computers to perform their intended tasks.

C. Discussion of how binary impacts the design and implementation of algorithms

Binary also affects the design and implementation of algorithms, as algorithms often rely on binary operations to process and manipulate data. The binary representation of data makes it possible for algorithms to perform complex operations and make decisions based on this data, enabling the development of advanced A.I. applications. Additionally, binary provides a universal language for computers to communicate with each other, allowing for the creation of distributed and parallel computing systems.

V. Conclusion

A. Recap of key points

In this chapter, we explored the basics of binary, including its definition and explanation, applications in computer hardware and software, and its role in A.I. We discussed how binary is central to computer science, including its impact on computer architecture and algorithm design and implementation.

B. Final thoughts on the importance of understanding binary in A.I.

Understanding binary is crucial for those interested in pursuing a career in A.I. or computer science. Without a solid understanding of binary, it is difficult to grasp the underlying mechanics of computer systems and the algorithms that drive A.I. applications.

C. Call to action for further exploration and learning.

The world of binary and computer science is vast and constantly evolving. To deepen your understanding of binary and its role in A.I., it is important to continue learning and exploring the topic. This may involve reading articles, taking online courses, or conducting independent research. With a strong foundation in binary, you will be well on your way to making a meaningful contribution to the field of A.I.

3

Applications of Binary in A.I.

I. Introduction

A. Overview of the chapter

This chapter will focus on the various applications of binary in the field of Artificial Intelligence (A.I.). Understanding the role of binary in A.I. is important as it forms the foundation for how computers store and process information, enabling the creation of complex algorithms and models.

B. Explanation of the importance of understanding binary in A.I. applications

Binary is critical in A.I. as it forms the basis of how computers represent and process information. This information is then used to train algorithms and models that are capable of performing complex tasks like image recognition, speech recognition, and robotics. Understanding binary, therefore, is essential for understanding the inner workings of A.I. and the applications it powers.

II. Machine Learning

A. Explanation of machine learning

Machine learning is a subset of A.I. that focuses on the development of algorithms and models that are capable of learning from data without being explicitly programmed. Machine learning algorithms are designed to improve their accuracy over time as they are exposed to more data.

B. Overview of binary in machine learning

1. Binary representation of data

In machine learning, data is often represented in binary form, allowing computers to process and store the information efficiently.

2. Binary optimization in machine learning algorithms

Binary optimization is a technique used in machine learning algorithms to improve their accuracy and efficiency. This is achieved by using binary values to represent the parameters of the algorithms, reducing the memory requirements and processing time.

C. Examples of binary-powered machine learning applications

1. Image classification

Image classification is a machine learning application that uses binary to process and classify images into different categories. This is achieved by using binary to represent the features of the images and optimizing the algorithms used to classify them.

2. Speech recognition

Speech recognition is a machine learning application that uses binary to process and transcribe spoken language into written text. This is achieved by using binary to represent the speech signals and optimizing the algorithms used to transcribe them.

III. Natural Language Processing

A. Explanation of natural language processing

Natural language processing (NLP) is a subfield of A.I. that focuses on the development of algorithms and models that can understand, interpret, and generate human language.

B. Overview of binary in natural language processing

1. Binary representation of text data

In NLP, text data is often represented in binary form, allowing computers to process and store the information efficiently.

2. Binary optimization in NLP algorithms

Binary optimization is a technique used in NLP algorithms to improve their accuracy and efficiency. This is achieved by using binary values to represent the parameters of the algorithms, reducing the memory requirements and processing time.

C. Examples of binary-powered NLP applications

1. Sentiment analysis

Sentiment analysis is an NLP application that uses binary to process and analyze the sentiment of text data. This is achieved by using binary to represent the features of the text data and optimizing the algorithms used to analyze the sentiment.

2. Text generation

Text generation is an NLP application that uses binary to generate text based on a given prompt. This is achieved by using binary to represent the prompt and optimizing the algorithms used to generate the text.

IV. Computer Vision

A. Explanation of computer vision

Computer vision is a subfield of A.I. that focuses on the development of algorithms and models that can understand and interpret visual information.

B. Overview of binary in computer vision

Binary plays a significant role in computer vision, specifically in the representation and processing of image data. Binary optimization is also used in computer vision algorithms to improve efficiency and accuracy.

1. Binary representation of image data

Binary representation of image data involves converting images into a series of bits that can be processed by computer systems. This allows computers to process images faster and more accurately, as well as store them more efficiently.

2. Binary optimization in computer vision algorithms

Binary optimization is applied to computer vision algorithms to improve their speed and accuracy. This includes the use of binary representations of image data in algorithms, as well as the optimization of algorithms using binary operations.

C. Examples of binary-powered computer vision applications

1. Object detection

Object detection is a computer vision application that uses algorithms to identify objects within images. Binary optimization is used to improve the accuracy and speed of object detection algorithms.

2. Image segmentation

Image segmentation is a computer vision application that involves dividing an image into different segments or regions, each of which represents a different object or background. Binary optimization is used in image segmentation algorithms to improve their efficiency and accuracy.

V. Robotics

A. Explanation of robotics

Robotics is a field that involves the design, construction, and operation of robots. Robotics is crucial in the development of advanced systems that can perform tasks that are dangerous or difficult for humans to carry out.

B. Overview of binary in robotics

Binary plays a crucial role in robotics by providing a convenient way to represent and process data for robotic systems. This includes the representation of sensor readings, control signals, and other data that is critical to the functioning of robots.

1. Binary representation of robotic data

In robotics, binary is used to represent sensor readings, control signals, and other data that is critical to the functioning of robots. This allows robots to process and store data in a compact and efficient manner.

2. Binary optimization in robotic algorithms

Binary also plays an important role in optimizing robotic algorithms. This involves the use of binary representations and operations to minimize the amount of memory and processing power required to carry out specific tasks.

C. Examples of binary-powered robotic applications

1. Autonomous navigation

Binary is used to represent and process data from sensors that are used for autonomous navigation. This includes data from cameras, LIDAR, and other sensors that are used to build maps and guide robots.

2. Motion planning

Binary is also used to optimize motion planning algorithms that are used to determine the path that a robot should follow. This involves the use of binary representations and operations to minimize the amount of memory and processing power required to plan and execute motions.

VI. Conclusion

A. Recap of key points

In this chapter, we have discussed the importance of binary in the field of robotics. We have explained how binary is used to represent and process data, as well as how binary optimization is used to improve the efficiency of robotic algorithms.

B. Final thoughts on the importance of understanding binary in A.I. applications

It is clear that binary plays a critical role in the development of advanced A.I. applications. A strong understanding of binary is essential for those who wish to work in the fields of robotics, machine learning, computer vision, and natural language processing.

C. Call to action for further exploration and learning.

We encourage you to continue your exploration and learning of binary and its applications in A.I. This includes reading more about the specific applications of binary in machine learning, computer vision, natural language processing, and robotics. By gaining a deeper understanding of binary, you will be well-equipped to contribute to the advancement of these fields.

4

Binary Coding for A.I.

I. Introduction

A. Overview of the chapter

This chapter will explore the topic of binary coding for A.I. applications. The chapter will provide an overview of binary coding, the importance of understanding binary coding in A.I., and provide guidance on how to code in binary for A.I. applications.

B. Explanation of the importance of binary coding in A.I.

Binary coding is the foundation of computer systems and A.I. applications. Understanding binary coding is essential for A.I. practitioners who want to build or work with intelligent systems. With a solid understanding of binary coding, A.I. practitioners can create more efficient algorithms, improve the performance of their systems, and debug and test their code more effectively.

II. How to Code in Binary for A.I.

A. Overview of binary coding

1. Explanation of binary coding languages

Binary coding can be done using various binary coding languages, such as Assembly, C++, and Python. Each language has its own syntax and structure, but the basic principles of binary coding remain the same.

2. Understanding binary code syntax and structure

In binary coding, instructions are written using binary digits, with each digit representing a binary value of either 0 or 1. The binary code is processed by the computer's processor, which reads the binary instructions and executes them accordingly. Understanding the syntax and structure of binary code is essential for writing efficient and effective code for A.I. applications.

B. Steps for writing binary code for A.I.

1. Defining the problem

The first step in writing binary code for A.I. applications is to define the problem that you are trying to solve. This will help you determine what kind of binary code you need to write and what algorithms you need to use.

2. Choosing a binary coding language

Once you have defined the problem, you will need to choose a binary coding language that is best suited for your needs. Consider factors such as the complexity of the problem, the amount of data you are working with, and the performance requirements of your system.

3. Writing the code

Once you have chosen a binary coding language, you can begin writing your code. Start by writing simple code that solves a small part of the problem, and gradually build up to more complex code that solves the entire problem.

4. Debugging and testing the code

As you write your code, it is important to test it and debug it to ensure that it is working as expected. This will help you identify any bugs or errors in your code and fix them before they cause more serious problems

III. Common Tools and Techniques for Binary Coding in A.I.

A. Overview of binary coding tools

1. Text editors

Text editors are the most basic tool for writing binary code. They provide a simple and straightforward way to write, edit, and save binary code.

2. Binary compilers

Binary compilers are tools that take binary code and translate it into machine code that can be executed by the computer's processor. They help you to write more efficient and optimized code, and can also help you identify and debug errors in your code.

3. Binary debuggers

Binary debuggers are tools that help you identify and debug errors in your binary code. They allow you to step through your code, watch variables, and inspect memory, making it easier to find and fix bugs.

B. Overview of binary coding techniques

1. Bit manipulation

Bit manipulation refers to the process of manipulating individual bits in binary code to perform various operations such as shifting, masking, or setting bits. This technique is commonly used in A.I. to optimize code performance or to manipulate data at a low level.

2. Binary arithmetic

Binary arithmetic involves performing mathematical operations on binary numbers, such as addition, subtraction, multiplication, and division. This is a crucial technique in A.I. as many algorithms and models use mathematical operations to process and analyze data.

3. Binary data structures

Binary data structures refer to data structures that are optimized for binary coding. These structures are designed to efficiently store and manipulate binary data, and are commonly used in A.I. for tasks such as data compression, data encryption, and indexing large amounts of data.

IV. Best Practices for Coding in Binary for A.I.

A. Explanation of best practices

1. Code readability and maintainability

When coding in binary for A.I., it is important to focus on code readability and maintainability. This involves writing clear and concise code that is easy to understand, modify, and maintain.

2. Optimization for performance

Performance optimization is a key aspect of coding in binary for A.I. This involves writing code that runs efficiently and makes the best use of available resources.

3. Error handling and debugging

Error handling and debugging are essential components of coding in binary for A.I. It is important to identify and fix errors early in the development process to ensure that the code works as intended.

B. Tips for writing efficient binary code for A.I.

1. Choosing the right data structures

Choosing the right data structures is crucial for writing efficient binary code for A.I. It is important to choose structures that are optimized for the specific task at hand and that can handle the volume and complexity of data.

2. Using optimization techniques

Using optimization techniques such as bit manipulation and binary arithmetic can help to improve the performance of binary code for A.I.

3. Writing clear and concise code

Writing clear and concise code is a best practice in binary coding for A.I. This involves writing code that is easy to understand and that minimizes the risk of errors and bugs.

V. Conclusion

A. Recap of key points

In this chapter, we discussed the importance of binary coding in A.I. and the steps and tools involved in coding in binary for A.I. applications. We covered the basics of binary coding languages, how to write binary code, and the common tools and techniques for binary coding in A.I. such as bit manipulation, binary arithmetic, and binary data structures. We also discussed the best practices for coding in binary for A.I., including code readability and maintainability, optimization for performance, and error handling and debugging.

B. Final thoughts on the importance of binary coding in A.I.

Binary coding is a critical aspect of A.I. and plays a significant role in the development and implementation of A.I. applications. A deep understanding of binary coding is essential for developing efficient, effective, and scalable A.I. systems.

C. Call to action for further exploration and learning.

If you are interested in learning more about binary coding for A.I., consider taking online courses or reading books and articles on the subject. Practicing writing binary code for different A.I. applications and experimenting with different tools and techniques will also help you deepen your understanding and improve your skills.

In conclusion, binary coding is a critical component of A.I. development, as it forms the basis of how computers process and analyze data. By understanding binary coding and following best practices, A.I. developers can write efficient and effective code that powers cutting-edge A.I. applications. To further explore and enhance your skills in binary coding for A.I., consider taking online courses, participating in coding challenges, or seeking out mentorship opportunities.

5

Advancements in Binary and A.I.

I. Introduction

A. Overview of the chapter

The chapter provides an overview of the ongoing advancements in binary and Artificial Intelligence (A.I.) and the impact they are having on the field.

B. Explanation of the ongoing advancements in binary and A.I.

Binary and A.I. have evolved significantly in recent years, with new trends and technologies emerging in the field. These advancements are improving the performance and efficiency of binary and A.I. systems, and opening up new application areas.

II. Emerging Trends in Binary and A.I.

A. Overview of emerging trends

1. Quantum computing

Quantum computing is a new trend in binary and A.I. that leverages the principles of quantum mechanics to perform calculations faster and more efficiently than classical computers.

2. Binary deep learning

Binary deep learning is a new trend that involves training deep neural networks with binary weights and activations, resulting in faster and more efficient models.

3. Binary generative models

Binary generative models are another emerging trend in binary and A.I. that use binary data structures to generate new data based on existing patterns.

B. Explanation of the impact of these trends on binary and A.I.

1. Improved performance

The emerging trends in binary and A.I. are improving the performance of these systems by reducing the time and computational resources required to perform tasks.

2. Increased efficiency

The advancements in binary and A.I. are also increasing the efficiency of these systems, enabling them to perform tasks faster and more accurately.

3. New application areas

The emerging trends in binary and A.I. are also opening up new application areas, such as quantum cryptography and binary deep learning, which are not possible with traditional binary and A.I. systems.

III. Future Directions for Research and Development

A. Overview of future directions

1. Integration of binary with other technologies

One of the future directions for research and development in binary and A.I. is the integration of binary with other technologies, such as quantum computing and deep learning, to create new and more advanced systems.

2. Development of new binary algorithms

Another future direction for research and development in binary and A.I. is the development of new binary algorithms to address specific tasks and improve performance.

3. Exploration of new application areas for binary and A.I.

Exploring new application areas for binary and A.I. is also a future direction for research and development, such as in areas like autonomous driving and natural language processing.

B. Explanation of the potential benefits of these future directions

1. Increased capabilities

The future directions in binary and A.I. research and development are expected to result in increased capabilities of these systems, enabling them to perform more complex tasks and solve more challenging problems.

2. Improved performance

The future directions for research and development in binary and A.I. are also expected to result in improved performance, with faster and more accurate systems.

3. Development of new solutions

The future directions for research and development in binary and A.I. are also expected to lead to the development of new solutions to address the needs of various industries and applications.

IV. How to Stay Updated on Advancements in Binary and A.I.

A. Overview of the importance of staying updated

Staying updated on the latest advancements in binary and A.I. is important to remain competitive and relevant in the field.

B. Resources for staying updated

1. Conferences and workshops

Attending conferences and workshops focused on binary and A.I. can provide an opportunity to hear from experts in the field and learn about the latest developments.

2. Journal articles and research papers

Reading journal articles and research papers in the field can help you stay up-to-date on the latest trends and advancements.

3. Online communities and forums

Participating in online communities and forums dedicated to binary and A.I. can provide a platform to connect with other professionals and discuss the latest developments.

C. Importance of continuous learning and professional development

Continuous learning and professional development are essential for staying updated and advancing in the field of binary and A.I. Attending workshops, taking online courses, and reading research papers are all ways to continually improve your knowledge and skills.

V. Conclusion

A. Recap of key points

In this chapter, we discussed the ongoing advancements in binary and A.I. We explored emerging trends, such as quantum computing, binary deep learning, and binary generative models, and how they are impacting the field. We also looked at future directions for research and development and the importance of staying updated on these advancements.

B. Final thoughts on the ongoing advancements in binary and A.I.

The advancements in binary and A.I. are constantly evolving, providing new and exciting opportunities for researchers, developers, and practitioners. These advancements have the potential to significantly improve performance, efficiency, and capabilities, leading to new solutions and applications.

C. Call to action for staying engaged and updated in the field.

It is important to stay engaged and updated in the field of binary and A.I. to stay competitive and relevant. There are many resources available, such as conferences, workshops, journal articles, online communities, and more, to help keep up-to-date on the latest advancements and developments. Continuous learning and professional development are also essential in this rapidly advancing field.

6

Debugging Binary Code for A.I.

I. Introduction

A. Overview of the chapter

This chapter provides an overview of the importance of debugging in binary coding for A.I. applications. It explains the common problems and errors encountered in binary coding and the techniques used to identify and fix these errors. Additionally, it highlights the best practices for debugging binary code and their benefits.

B. Explanation of the importance of debugging in binary coding for A.I.

Debugging is a crucial step in the development of A.I. applications as it helps to identify and correct errors in the code. These errors can range from syntax errors to logical errors, semantic errors, and run-time errors, which can have a significant impact on the performance, accuracy, and stability of the application. As such, it is important for developers to have a thorough understanding of debugging techniques and best practices to ensure that their A.I. applications run smoothly.

II. Common Problems and Errors in Binary Coding for A.I.

A. Overview of common problems and errors

1. Syntax errors

These are errors in the syntax or structure of the code that prevent it from being executed.

2. Logical errors

These are errors in the logic or reasoning of the code, causing it to produce incorrect results.

3. Semantic errors

These are errors in the meaning or interpretation of the code, causing it to produce unexpected results.

4. Run-time errors

These are errors that occur while the code is being executed, such as memory leaks or buffer overflows.

B. Explanation of the impact of these problems and errors on A.I. applications

1. Reduced performance

Errors in the code can cause the application to run slower, reducing its overall performance.

2. Incorrect results

Errors in the logic or reasoning of the code can cause it to produce incorrect results, affecting the accuracy of the application.

3. System crashes

Run-time errors can cause the application to crash, resulting in data loss and system instability.

III. Techniques for Identifying and Fixing Errors

A. Overview of techniques for identifying and fixing errors

1. Debugging tools and software

There are a range of tools and software available for debugging code, such as debuggers, profilers, and memory analyzers.

2. Code inspections and code reviews

A code inspection is a manual review of the code to identify errors, while a code review is a more comprehensive examination that involves multiple developers.

3. Automated testing and continuous integration

Automated testing and continuous integration can help to identify and fix errors in the code early on in the development process.

B. Explanation of how these techniques can be applied to binary coding for A.I.

1. Improved efficiency

Debugging tools and software can help to identify and fix errors in the code quickly, improving the efficiency of the development process.

2. Increased accuracy

Code inspections and code reviews can help to improve the accuracy of the code by identifying errors that might have been missed by automated testing.

3. Faster time to market

Automated testing and continuous integration can help to identify and fix errors early on in the development process, reducing the time to market.

IV. Best Practices for Debugging Binary Code

A. Overview of best practices

1. Adherence to coding standards

Adhering to coding standards can help to reduce the number of errors in the code and make it easier to debug.

2. Use of version control systems

Using version control systems can help to track changes to the code and make it easier to revert to previous versions if needed.

3. Regular code inspections

Regular code inspections can help to identify and fix early in the development process, reducing the time and effort required to debug the code.

B. Explanation of the benefits of following these best practices

1. Improved quality of code

Following best practices can result in higher-quality code that is easier to maintain and debug.

2. Increased efficiency

Debugging is faster and easier when best practices are followed, reducing the time and effort required to resolve issues.

3. Reduced risk of errors

Following best practices can help to prevent errors from occurring in the first place, reducing the risk of errors in the code.

V. Conclusion

A. Recap of key points

In this chapter, we have discussed the importance of debugging in binary coding for A.I. and the common problems and errors that can arise. We have also discussed various techniques for identifying and fixing errors, including the use of debugging tools and software, code inspections and code reviews, and automated testing and continuous integration. Additionally, we have explored best practices for debugging binary code, including adherence to coding standards, use of version control systems, and regular code inspections.

B. Final thoughts on the importance of debugging in binary coding for A.I.

Debugging is an essential part of the development process and is crucial to the success of A.I. applications. By following best practices and utilizing effective debugging techniques, developers can ensure that their code is of high quality, efficient, and free of errors.

C. Call to action for developing a robust and efficient debugging process.

It is important for developers to stay updated on the latest advancements in debugging and to continually improve their debugging processes. This can be done by attending conferences and workshops, reading journal articles and research papers, and participating in online communities and forums. Continuous learning and professional development can also help to ensure that developers are equipped with the skills

and knowledge needed to debug binary code effectively and
efficiently.

7

Binary and Ethics in A.I.

I. Introduction

A. Overview of the chapter

This chapter focuses on the intersection of binary and ethics in Artificial Intelligence (A.I.). It aims to provide an overview of the growing concern around ethics in A.I. and the impact of binary on privacy and security.

B. Explanation of the growing concern around ethics in A.I.

As A.I. becomes more prevalent and integrated into various aspects of our lives, it's becoming increasingly important to consider the ethical implications of its development and deployment. Ethical considerations include issues such as fairness and equality, responsibility and accountability, and transparency and interpretability.

II. The Impact of Binary on Privacy and Security in A.I.

A. Overview of the impact of binary on privacy and security

Binary coding plays a critical role in the privacy and security of A.I. systems. It affects the protection of sensitive data, protection against cyber threats, and user privacy.

1. Sensitive data protection

Binary code is used to manage and store sensitive data, making it crucial for protecting this data from unauthorized access.

2. Protection against cyber threats

Binary code is used to develop security measures that help protect against cyber threats such as hacking and malware.

3. User privacy

Binary code is used to manage and control access to user data, making it essential for protecting user privacy.

B. Explanation of the potential risks of poor binary coding practices in A.I.

Poor binary coding practices can result in data breaches, system vulnerabilities, and unintended consequences. These can have serious implications for privacy and security, and it's essential to implement robust measures to mitigate these risks.

1. Data breaches

Poorly written binary code can leave sensitive data vulnerable to breaches, leading to significant harm to both individuals and organizations.

2. System vulnerabilities

Poor binary coding can result in system vulnerabilities that can be exploited by cyber criminals to steal sensitive data or gain unauthorized access to systems.

3. Unintended consequences

Poorly written binary code can also result in unintended consequences, such as systems behaving in unexpected or harmful ways.

III. Ethical Considerations in the Development and Deployment of A.I.

A. Overview of ethical considerations

The development and deployment of A.I. involves a range of ethical considerations, including bias and discrimination, responsibility and accountability, and transparency and interpretability. These considerations impact the fairness and equality of A.I. systems, public trust, and their social impact.

1. Bias and discrimination

Artificial intelligence systems can perpetuate existing biases and discriminatory practices, making it important to ensure that they are designed and developed with fairness and equality in mind.

2. Responsibility and accountability

With the increasing power of A.I., it is important to consider who is responsible and accountable for the actions of these systems.

3. Transparency and interpretability

Artificial intelligence systems can be difficult to understand and interpret, making it important to ensure that they are transparent and interpretable in their decision-making processes.

B. Explanation of how these considerations impact the development and deployment of A.I.

The ethical considerations mentioned above must be taken into account in the development and deployment of A.I. systems. Failure to do so could result in a loss of public trust, decreased social responsibility, and the use of A.I. in an irresponsible manner.

1. Fairness and equality

Ensuring that A.I. systems are fair and equal in their decision-making processes helps to promote public trust and increase social responsibility.

2. Public trust

A.I. systems that are transparent and interpretable in their decision-making processes are more likely to engender public trust and support.

3. Social impact

The development and deployment of A.I. systems can have a significant impact on society, making it important to consider the social implications of their use.

IV. Best Practices for Responsible Use of Binary in A.I.

A. Overview of best practices

To ensure the responsible use of A.I., it's essential to follow best practices, such as ethical by design, robust privacy and security measures, and transparent decision-making processes.

1. Ethical by design

This approach prioritizes ethics at every stage of the development process, from planning to deployment. It ensures that A.I. systems are designed with the end-user in mind and are built to promote ethical outcomes.

2. Robust privacy and security measures

A.I. systems process and store vast amounts of data, making privacy and security critical concerns. Robust privacy and security measures help to protect sensitive data, prevent cyber threats, and ensure the privacy of users.

3. Transparent decision-making processes

A.I. systems make decisions based on algorithms and data, and it's important that these decision-making processes are transparent and interpretable. This enables organizations to understand how and why A.I. systems are making certain decisions and to identify and address any biases or unfairness.

B. Explanation of the benefits of following these best practices

By following these best practices, organizations can improve public trust, increase social responsibility, and ensure the robust and responsible use of A.I.

1. Improved public trust

By prioritizing ethics and transparency, organizations can build public trust in A.I. systems, which is crucial for promoting their adoption and use.

2. Increased social responsibility

Adhering to best practices helps organizations to be more socially responsible, which can improve their reputation and contribute to the responsible development and deployment of A.I. systems.

3. Robust and responsible use of A.I.

By following these best practices, organizations can ensure that A.I. systems are robust and responsibly used, which can promote their continued development and deployment.

V. Conclusion

A. Recap of key points

This chapter has provided an overview of the growing concern around ethics in A.I. and the impact of binary on privacy and security. It has also discussed ethical considerations in the development and deployment of A.I. and best practices for responsible use of binary in A.I.

B. Final thoughts on the importance of ethics in binary coding for A.I.

It's crucial to consider the ethical implications of the development and deployment of A.I. and to follow best practices to ensure its responsible use. Binary coding plays a critical role in this process and must be carefully considered.

C. Call to action for responsible development and deployment of A.I.

This chapter serves as a call to action for organizations and individuals involved in the development and deployment of A.I. to be mindful of the ethical implications and to follow best practices for responsible use.

8

Binary and the Future of A.I.

I. Introduction

A. Overview of the chapter

In this chapter, we will explore the role of binary in shaping the future of artificial intelligence (A.I.), as well as the potential impact of emerging technologies and innovations. The chapter will conclude with a discussion of the exciting potential for binary to transform and improve our world

B. Explanation of the importance of understanding the future of binary and A.I.

Binary is a fundamental aspect of A.I., as it provides a way to encode information and perform computations. Therefore, understanding the future of binary and A.I. is important for those working in technology and for society as a whole. This knowledge will allow us to anticipate and prepare for the impact of future developments, as well as to consider ethical and societal implications.

II. The Role of Binary in Shaping the Future of A.I.

A. Overview of binary's role in shaping the future of A.I.

Binary plays a critical role in shaping the future of A.I. in several ways:

1. Driving advancements in technology

Binary provides a way to perform complex computations, and advancements in binary technology have driven advancements in A.I.

2. Enabling new applications

Binary enables the development of new A.I. applications, such as image and speech recognition.

3. Influencing ethical considerations

The use of A.I. has ethical implications, and binary technology can influence the development of ethical considerations.

B. Explanation of how binary will continue to shape the future of A.I.

Binary will continue to shape the future of A.I. through:

1. Advancements in hardware and software

Advances in hardware and software will allow for more efficient binary processing and more complex A.I. computations.

2. Development of new coding practices

New coding practices will emerge that take advantage of binary technology and drive further advancements in A.I.

3. Integration with emerging technologies

The integration of binary with emerging technologies, such as quantum computing and edge computing, will enable new and more powerful A.I. applications.

III. Emerging Technologies and Innovations in Binary and A.I.

A. Overview of emerging technologies

There are several emerging technologies that will impact binary and A.I., including:

1. Quantum computing

Quantum computing uses quantum-mechanical phenomena to perform computations, offering the potential for significant advancements in binary processing and A.I.

2. Edge computing

Edge computing involves processing data close to the source of data, offering the potential for more efficient A.I. computations and real-time applications.

3. Neuromorphic computing

Neuromorphic computing involves creating computing systems that are modeled after the structure and function of the human brain, offering the potential for more efficient A.I. computations and new applications.

B. Explanation of how these technologies will impact binary and A.I.

These emerging technologies will impact binary and A.I. by:

1. Improved performance and efficiency

The use of these technologies will lead to improved performance and efficiency in binary processing and A.I. computations.

2. New application areas

These technologies will enable new applications in areas such as healthcare, finance, and transportation.

3. Advancements in ethical considerations

The integration of these technologies with binary and A.I. will raise new ethical considerations, and advancements in these technologies will influence the development of ethical considerations.

IV. The Potential for Binary to Transform Industries and Society

A. Overview of the potential for binary to transform industries and society

1. Healthcare

Binary can be used to improve healthcare services by automating tasks and providing more accurate diagnoses. It can also be used to analyze large amounts of patient data to identify patterns and improve treatments.

2. Finance

Binary can transform the finance industry by improving efficiency, reducing costs, and reducing the risk of fraud. It can also be used to analyze financial data to identify patterns and make better investment decisions.

3. Transportation

Binary can revolutionize transportation by automating tasks, improving safety, and reducing costs. It can also be used to analyze traffic data to optimize routes and reduce congestion.

B. Explanation of the benefits of these transformations

1. Improved quality of life

By transforming industries and society, binary can help to improve quality of life by making services more efficient, reducing costs, and improving safety.

2. Economic growth

The transformations brought about by binary can also lead to economic growth by creating new jobs and improving productivity.

3. Increased productivity

Binary can increase productivity by automating tasks and reducing the risk of human error. It can also be used to analyze
data to identify trends and make more informed decisions.

V. Conclusion

A. Recap of key points

In this chapter, we have explored the potential for binary to
transform industries and society. By improving healthcare,
finance, and transportation, binary has the potential to improve
quality of life, promote economic growth, and increase productivity.

B. Final thoughts on the future of binary and A.I.

The future of binary and A.I. is bright, with the potential to bring
about significant positive change in our world. It is important
that we continue to develop and implement best practices for
responsible use of binary to ensure that these transformations
are beneficial for all.

C. Discussion of the exciting potential for binary to transform and improve our world.

The use of binary in A.I. has the potential to transform and improve our world in a number of ways. By automating tasks, reducing costs, and improving safety, binary has the potential to improve quality of life and promote economic growth. It is an exciting time for the future of binary and A.I., and we look forward to seeing the positive impact it will have on our world.

9

Career Opportunities in Binary and A.I.

I. Introduction

A. Overview of the chapter

The field of binary and artificial intelligence is rapidly growing and there is a growing demand for professionals in this field. This chapter will provide an overview of the job opportunities, skills and qualifications needed, and resources for learning and professional development in the field of binary and A.I.

B. Explanation of the growing demand for professionals in the field of binary and A.I.

The use of binary and artificial intelligence is becoming increasingly widespread in various industries, leading to a growing demand for professionals who are skilled in these areas. Companies are looking for individuals who can help them develop and implement A.I. systems, design and implement machine learning algorithms, and analyze and interpret data.

II. Job Opportunities in the Field of Binary and A.I.

A. Overview of job opportunities

There are several job opportunities available in the field of binary and A.I. including software engineers, data scientists, and machine learning engineers.

1. *Software engineers* are responsible for developing and maintaining A.I. systems.
2. *Data scientists* are responsible for designing and implementing machine learning algorithms.
3. *Machine learning engineers* are responsible for analyzing and interpreting data.

B. Explanation of the duties and responsibilities of these roles

1. Developing and maintaining A.I. systems

Software engineers are responsible for developing and maintaining A.I. systems. They ensure that the systems are functional, efficient, and secure.

2. Designing and implementing machine learning algorithms

Data scientists are responsible for designing and implementing machine learning algorithms. They use statistical methods and algorithms to analyze data and develop models that can be used to make predictions.

3. Analyzing and interpreting data

Machine learning engineers are responsible for analyzing and interpreting data. They use statistical methods and algorithms to analyze data and make predictions.

III. Skills and Qualifications Needed for a Career in Binary and A.I.

A. Overview of required skills and qualifications

1. Strong coding skills

2. Knowledge of machine learning and data science

3. Understanding of binary and computer science

B. Explanation of how these skills and qualifications impact job performance

1. Ability to develop and implement A.I. systems

Strong coding skills are essential for developing and implement-ing A.I. systems.

2. Ability to analyze and interpret data

Knowledge of machine learning and data science is essential for analyzing and interpreting data.

3. Ability to stay current with advancements in the field

Understanding of binary and computer science is important for staying current with advancements in the field.

IV. Resources for Learning and Professional Development

A. Overview of resources for learning and professional development

There are several resources available for learning and professional development in the field of binary and A.I., including:

1. Online courses

2. Professional organizations

3. Industry conferences

B. Explanation of how these resources can support career growth

1. Continuous learning and skill development

Online courses and professional organizations provide opportunities for continuous learning and skill development

2. Networking opportunities

Industry conferences provide opportunities for networking with other professionals in the field.

3. Exposure to industry advancements and innovations

Industry conferences provide exposure to industry advancements and innovations.

V. Conclusion

A. Recap of key points

This chapter provided an overview of the job opportunities, skills and qualifications needed, and resources for learning and professional development in the field of binary and A.I.

B. Final thoughts on the opportunities for a career in binary and A.I.

As technology continues to advance, the demand for professionals in the field of binary and A.I. will only increase. There is a wealth of job opportunities available, including software engineering, data science, and machine learning engineering. These roles require strong coding skills, knowledge of machine learning and data science, and an understanding of binary and computer science.

C. Discussion of the exciting potential for growth and impact in this field.

A career in binary and A.I. has the potential for tremendous growth and impact. This field is at the forefront of technological innovation and has the potential to transform and improve industries and society as a whole. The opportunities for continuous learning and skill development, as well as exposure to industry advancements and innovations, make this an exciting field to be a part of. Overall, a career in binary and A.I. offers the potential for personal and professional growth, as well as the ability to make a positive impact on the world.

10

Conclusion

I. Recap of Key Points

In this chapter, we have summarized the key points covered in the previous chapters of "A.I. and the Art of Binary". We will cover the importance of understanding binary in the field of A.I. and the various applications and uses of binary in A.I.

A. Explanation of A.I. and binary

We have discussed the basics of binary, including its definition, how it works in A.I., and its relationship with computer science.

B. Applications of binary in A.I.

We have explored the different applications of binary in A.I., including machine learning, natural language processing, computer vision, and robotics.

C. Binary coding for A.I.

We have discussed how to code in binary for A.I., the tools and techniques used, and best practices for coding.

D. Advancements in binary and A.I.

We have looked at the emerging trends and future directions in binary and A.I. and the impact of binary on privacy, security, and ethics in A.I.

E. Career Opportunities in Binary and A.I.

We have discussed the job opportunities and skills required for a career in binary and A.I. and resources for learning and professional development.

II. Final Thoughts on the Future of Binary and A.I.

In this section, we have reflected on the future of binary and A.I. and the role of binary in shaping the future of A.I. We have discussed the potential for binary to transform industries and society and the emerging technologies and innovations in binary and A.I.

III. Call to Action for Further Exploration and Learning

Finally, we have encouraged the reader to continue exploring and learning about binary and A.I. We have suggested resources for further learning and provided guidance on how to stay updated on advancements in binary and A.I..

In conclusion, understanding binary is crucial for anyone interested in A.I. and its applications. By gaining a deeper understanding of binary, individuals can expand their careers, explore new technologies, and contribute to the development of A.I. in responsible and ethical ways.

About the Author

Avery Wright brings a unique and important perspective to the world of AI. With a focus on the ethical, legal, and social implications, Avery provides valuable insights and inspiration to those interested in this rapidly-evolving technology.

You can connect with me on:

🌐 https://sirexodia.wixsite.com/avery-wright

🐦 https://twitter.com/AveryWrightAI

📘 https://www.facebook.com/profile.php?id=100089987171726

Subscribe to my newsletter:

✉ https://sirexodia.wixsite.com/avery-wright

Also by Avery Wright

"A.I. and the Art of Binary" is a comprehensive guide that covers the basics of binary, its applications in A.I., coding in binary for A.I., advancements and trends, and career opportunities in the field. Written by Avery Wright, a veteran in the field of artificial intelligence, the book delves into the ethical, legal, and social implications of this technology and provides valuable insights and inspiration to readers interested in this rapidly evolving field.

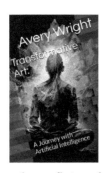

Transformative Art - A Journey with Artificial Intelligence
Transformative Art: A Journey with AI is a visually stunning and thought-provoking book that explores the intersection of artificial intelligence and the world of art. The book features breathtaking images of futuristic cities, technology, vehicles, robots, flying ships, conceptual art, abstract art, and unique pieces, all within the context of transformative art. Each chapter begins with a powerful quote that sets the tone for a deep dive into the themes of perception, change, reflection, risk-taking, emotional connection, the journey within, and the universal language of art. The book is written by Avery Wright, a talented author with a passion for exploring the ways in which technology is changing our lives and our world. This book is a must-read for anyone interested in the intersection of art, technology, and the human experience. https://www.amazon.com/dp/B0BTWNYLJD